URBAN TALES OF THE BIBLE: SHORT STORY SERIES BOOK 2 - THE WUSSY KING AND THE EVIL BOSS QUEEN

Written by T.S. HOLDER
May 8, 2022

Printed in the United States of America

ISBN 9798-9854404-4-7

This book series is dedicated to all of the elders in my family line. Those that have gone before us and those that are still here. Thank you for leaving a strong and powerful legacy of loving Yeshua.

If you would like TS Holder to do a live reading and/or for autographed copies email TS Holder at Suprnatrl@gmail.com and put TS Holder - Live Reading or TS Holder - Autographed Copies in the subject line.

Introduction

In today's society we see magazine articles and television shows about how so many Boss Queens are doing their thing and owning their destiny. There are restaurants named Boss Queens, some spell Queens with a double S, there are clothing stores named Boss Queens and there is even a website titled Boss Queens Bible and there is a song titled Boss Queen!

The urban term boss is normally used to describe a person that has control of their life and is walking in their destiny, has financial security, is a leader, has strong character and does what it takes to ensure that their money is working for them. The boss makes moves and does the most!! Now let's apply that to a female. She is someone that cultivates any relationship that she is in, is an atmosphere changer and when she walks in the room she commands the room's energy! She only walks in positivity, is a leader and she knows how to handle her business and any and everything pertaining to her life. That makes her a Boss Queen!

Now when this same Boss Queen is in a love relationship not only does she love hard and bring the man's standards up, but she is very protective of who or what she considers to be hers and who enters that circle. So in this short story we will witness an Evil Boss Queen who works it to the ultimate degree.

When we are in a love relationship we want our significant other to have everything that they want in life, but we should have limits on what we will do to make sure that they are spoiled rotten! Not this Boss Queen, she has no limits and takes it way too far, does too much and lets nothing stand in her way up to and including taking out the person coming against her man and who is stopping him from getting what he wants! This Evil Boss Queen is so far off the chain that the chain links broke!

The book cover title is not a typo. As you will find out this is no ordinary queen. She is evil, emasculating and extra and because of this she deserves an extra E. She is not a proper Queen, she is a Queeen!!

Let us get into this story, so put your feet up, get a nice warm blankey and of course something to munch and snack on, along with your drink of choice! Are you ready to let these pages talk to you and weave the story of the Wussy King and an Evil Boss Queen? Then let's get it!

2 Kings 1 – The Wussy King and the Evil Boss Queen

This is a story of a king, an evil king to be more specific, who just didn't know when it was time to quit the dumb stuff that his family taught him. The king that ruled at this time was King Ahaziah. Before we move forward in the story it will be a good thing for us to know this king's background and his family history. Yes, we are about to do a background check on King Ahaziah.

The first step in this background check will be to find out who King Ahaziah's people are. He is the son of King Ahab and Queen Jezebel. Now I know that some of y'all, if not most of y'all have heard of Queen Jezebel! Yes, Jezebel's name gets a lot of airplay in the pulpit! I would go so far to say that it's probably one of the most preached about names in the history of sermons! There are so many books about this woman that I would like to say STOP IT! I really do believe that we got the picture! Anywho, if by chance you have not heard of Queen Jezebel I will introduce her to you a little further into this background check. Alright let's get into this!

King Ahaziah is the brother of the wicked, back-biting, scheming, stone cold murderer Queen Mother the Demon Athaliah, who is featured in book one of this short story series titled the Prophet & The Ho'. King Ahab is Queen Jezebel's man and Ahaziah's father. He is also the CEO and founder of the Omri Dynasty. It is named the Omri Dynasty after Ahab's father Omri. This evil dynasty ruled for about 50 years! Can you imagine what it would be like today if we had one president in office for the next 50 years? I am so glad that we don't have to find that out.

King Ahab was a pretty spineless and weak at heart. It was his wife Queen Jezebel that handled business and held things down. She didn't like nobody messing with her man Ahab. For example in 1 Kings 21:1-29 Ahab wanted a particular piece of land that was a vineyard and was owned by a man named Naboth who lived in the city of Jezreel. (Remember the name Jezreel from book one?)

When Ahab asked to buy the vineyard at a fair price, Naboth decided that the land should stay with his family. Which he had every right to do! He probably wanted to leave it as a family legacy for future generations, ya know, generational wealth.

Well, that was the wrong answer to give Ahab and especially since he had a wife like Boss Queen Jezebel. Ahab got all in his feelings, ran home and went to bed all depressed, and feeling some kind of way.

Evil Boss Queen Jezebel went into the room to find out what was wrong with her man. When Ahab told her what was going on she just wasn't having it. Nobody was going to make her man, the king, feel some type of way. Jezebel asked Ahab, "Bae, what's up with you? Why you in the bed, crying and things?"

Ahab said, "There is a vineyard that I want. I tried to buy it from Naboth and with ten toes down he told me no. Who says no to the king?"

Jezebel said, "Well, bae, you are the king! Why didn't you just take it?"

Ahab said, "I couldn't do that. I'm tryna be fair and honest."

Jezebel said, "Fair and honest! Man get up outta that bed and be THE KING that I know you are. I will show you how to get the land that you want and that you deserve. Whatever my honey wants, my honey gets! YOU DA KING!! OH NO, don't NOBODY tell my baby NO. Who does Naboth think that he is? He got the wrong King today baby!"

Then the evil boss queen said to herself, " I must set a precedent, ya know set an example, better yet make an example out of Naboth in this matter so that it does not happen again!! After this no one will ever tell my man NO again! I got work to do!"

Ahab didn't move from the bed. He stayed curled up in the fetal position, sucking his thumb like a big baby! But Jezebel, chile evil boss queen Jezebel was on it like red on hot sauce! Yes, she was hot and about to take care of business like the Evil Boss Queen she was.

Jezebel was a sinister woman and many women today are told that they have a Jezebel spirit because they are a boss and know how to run things. There is nothing wrong with being a boss, but there is a lot wrong with being plain old evil, whether you are a male or female! And while I am at it why is it that there aren't as many sermons preached about how weak and spineless Ahab was? That tells me something right there.

Jezebel sat down at the Royal Computer and began to send out emails to the Mayor and Councilmen of Jezreel from Ahab's Royal Email Account. In this email she said, "Dear sirs, this is your King, King Ahab and I want to call a day of fasting and prayer and I want to choose one of Jezreel's finest to lead the people in this fast. I want Naboth to be the leader of this day of fasting and prayer. Also, I want you to find two crack heads that have the worst reputation in Jezreel. I want you to find the crack heads who will do anything for their next fix and when you have found them I want them sitting right across from Naboth. These two men must not have a single bone of honesty or integrity in them. They must be all about getting that money so that they can get their next fix AND they must be willing to do anything to get their next fix. Tell these two men that once they are in place and the fast starts but before the praying starts, to say the following words and that they must say these words so loud that everyone will hear them. Tell them to say that Naboth is not an honest man and that he is spreading rumors about the king and god. Now, once these two no count crack heads have said this you must have the po-po take Naboth out and kill him. There is a new law in place that has brought back death by firing squad because we can't get the drugs for lethal injection. Naboth will be the first one to be killed in this manner."

It was less than 24 hours that after the emails hit the Royal IT Servers the entire plan was carried out. The hardest thing that the Mayor had to do was to figure out which two crack heads to choose! That was a task in itself because most crackheads have mood swings, and all of them are about doing what it takes to get their next fix and the main thing is that they are paranoid! So the Mayor had to convince these crackheads that he was for real. That it was not a setup just to get them off the streets and into rehab. The Mayor also had to have someone to watch them because crackheads will steal your feet out of your shoes and find someone to buy your feet and shoes, if you are not careful!

Booooyyyy I'll tell you, Evil Boss Queen is setting Naboth up for the fall in a Royal way. Poor

Naboth didn't even know what was coming his way. Bruh didn't stand a chance!!

The Mayor sent word to Naboth saying, "We are declaring a day of fasting and prayer and we would like for you to lead this special day. We chose you because you are an upstanding citizen in this community of Jezreel and the people look up to you as a leader so we want to extend this honor to you. We certainly hope that you would consider this offer and accept the honor of leading this special day of fasting and prayer. Ya know the Bible says that certain things can only come out and be destroyed by fasting and prayer and with what our city is facing today in the way of this crack, opioid and Fentanyl epidemic we need fasting and prayer. We also want you to know that we have chosen two of the city's worst crackheads to sit on the podium with you. In this way when the power of God hits these two crackheads all will see what prayer and fasting can do. Please respond as soon as possible, because we want to start this today."

After Naboth read the email, his heart started beating fast and he was too excited. He thought to himself, "Finally, finally someone sees that I am a man of God and that I have been living a righteous life. God I thank you!"

Naboth ran to his wife and said, "Honey, honey, look! Come and see this email that I just received from the Mayor saying that there is going to be a day of fasting and prayer and they want me to lead it!! Wow!! Honey, they recognize that I am a leader in the community and the people look up to me!"

Naboth's wife said, "Honey that is great. You have been wanting to make a difference in the community and leave a legacy. I guess that your prayers have been answered, but do you think that we should first pray and ask God if He wants you to do this? After all when we prayed last night and this morning God said nothing to either of us about a day of fasting and prayer. You know how this government is, shouldn't we be on the safe side and ask God first? I think that we should. I feel it in my spirit that we should seek God first in this as we do in all things"

Naboth had been tricked and didn't even recognize the tactic being used against him was one that appealed to his spiritual ego. The enemy knew exactly where to hit Naboth to pull him into a scheme that would take his life.

Notice how the Mayor did not say that the King wanted a day of fasting, because if he had Naboth would have known that this was a trick. King Ahab and Evil Boss Queen Jezebel were known worshippers of Baal. (Baal is the Canaanite god who is the enemy of Yahuah our God)

Just the fact that a day of prayer and fasting was called should have been a hint that something was off because almost the entire kingdom was into Baal worship. Naboth should have thought that this was all too suspect as his wife did. He should have taken the time to seek God on this matter. Everything that sounds good certainly ain't good.

Naboth's ego got in the way. He should have taken the time to inquire of God before accepting the offer and then he would have known what was up.

Naboth ran back to his computer and accepted the offer without any further delay. He was more than happy to lead out in a day of prayer and fasting. Afterwards he started fasting but did not have time to pray because he had to head on over to the staging area. How did he think that he could lead in prayer if he was not prayed up himself!

The Mayor emailed who he thought was King Ahab and said, "Everything is in place. Naboth has accepted the offer to lead the day of prayer and fasting and is on his way here as I type this reply message. Oh yeah, I finally found the city's worst two crackheads and we will start the services shortly. This will be live streamed so that all can see just what will happen to anyone speaking against the King and god!"

Jezebel, posing as King Ahab replied, "I love it when a plan comes together. I will be watching the live stream. All thanks to Baal!"

The Mayor went live and within a few hours Naboth was dead and everyone in Jezreel and the surrounding area watched his death by firing squad as it took place! Chile, people were talking up a storm and saying, "How could those two crackheads lie on Naboth like that and how could the Mayor take the word of two known crackheads as being legit, over a good God fearing man like Naboth? This just ain't right!"

Another could be heard saying, "Man, this was a set-up by the New World Order. If this is how they treated Naboth, we don't stand a chance!"

Preachers in the town called a special meeting so that they could pray over the people and give them hope. The biggest meeting was held at Mt. Moriah Missionary Bapti-presbyteri-costal A.M.E., C.M.E. primitive holiness church of Jezreel. Most of the people attended this service and heard the sermon titled, "Are you Ready" being preached. Someone else said that over at First Corinthians Non-Denominational Church of Jezreel the sermon was, "It could happen to you in the twinkling of an eye."

Some of the holiness women ran over to see about Naboth's wife and children to see what they

21

could do to help them out in this bad sit-chu-mation. They knew that she had to be scared for her life and needed some support.

As soon as Evil Queen Boss Jezebel saw that her plan had been executed and the coast was clear for her man to go get his vineyard, she went running into the bedroom where Ahab was still in bed like a little two year old in the fetal position. Jezebel said, "Honey get up! Get up! Naboth is dead. I just saw it on live stream. It seems that he said some pretty nasty things about you and god and he was killed by firing squad for all to see. Get up!"

Ahab turned over and said, "Gurl, don't be playin' with me right now. I ain't in the mood."

Jezebel said, "Naw, this is for real, for real. Get up!"

Ahab jumped outta bed, ran to the live stream where it was being replayed over and over and he looked at Jezebel and said, "You did this didn't you? This is YOUR style!"

Jezebel said, "Bae for you, there is nothing that I wouldn't do. So go on out there and get that vineyard and bring me back a bottle of premium sweet red wine, please and thank you."

Well Ahab and especially Jezebel didn't add God into this equation! God spoke to the Prophet Elijah who had a known reputation for being on point when speaking on God's behalf. He did not miss a beat. If he said God said it, it happened just as he said it would. God spoke to Elijah and said, "Elijah, that degum Evil Boss Queen Jezebel is at it again! She has out done herself this time."

Elijah said, "NAAAWWW, not Jezebel again!"

God said, "Yes, she just doesn't get it! I need you to go to the vineyard that Naboth owns because Jezebel put a plot together and has had Naboth killed and Ahab is getting ready to go take control of Naboth's vineyard. Jezebel has even put in an order for a bottle of premium sweet red wine! She is just ruthless!"

Elijah said, "That hussy is really something. So what's the plan Lord?"

God said, "Go down there and tell Ahab, so you think that your crazy wife's plan has worked. First Jezebel has Naboth killed and now you think that you can just walk on over there and take his vineyard, his family's legacy and generational wealth? Naboth said no and that he would not sell it to you, so now you think that you can just waltz your narrow behind over there and take it? The same way that you have killed Naboth and the dogs are licking his blood, they will also lick your blood and anyone in your family that dies. Yes, the dogs will also lick your family's blood. The Lord will utterly destroy you and your family and there will be no one from the Omri Dynasty left. You knew what Jezebel did was evil and instead of you manning up and taking control over the situation, you are going right along with it. If your family member dies in the city the dogs will lick their blood, if they die out side of the city the birds will eat them."

Elijah went down to find Ahab and told him exactly what God said. How do you think that you would react if you heard this about you and your family? Well, chile look-a-here, when Ahab heard those words from the Prophet Elijah, oh boy started his own personal time of fasting and went straight into a place of repentance. He did this with a quickness! Now Ahab might have been a Baal worshiper, but he knew just like everyone else did, that if Prophet Elijah came and brought you a Word from God that you could take it to the Royal Bank and cash it because it was gonna happen. Oh yeah, it was gonna happen!

Ahab tore his clothes off and put on some black clothes to show that he was repenting, mourning and fasting. The look on his face was like he had eaten some bad food and his stomach was tore up. Oh boy wasn't ready to die just yet. He was trying to mend his evil ways, but what was he going to do about Jezebel, she was the worst and she was the seat of his problems? He knew that he didn't have the strength or mental ability to outsmart her or to tell her to let him lead. She wasn't about that life!

God even noticed how Ahab was touched by the Word from Prophet Elijah and trying to straighten up. God said to Elijah, "My word really struck Ahab's heart. He has really taken it to heart and is trying to straighten himself out and not ride

27

so hard with his Evil Boss Queen Jezebel, who definitely does the most. Now, because he has done this I will not destroy his family while he is alive, but when his son Ahaziah becomes king I will do it then."

It was about 3 years later that a war broke out and Ahab ignored the word of the prophet who said not to go to war, and just as sure as he ignored Prophet Micaiah's word and went into battle he was killed. When he died his son Ahaziah became the 8th king of the northern Kingdom of Israel at the age of 22. He was just like his father Ahab and his mother Jezebel, just one evil man that made all of Israel sin against God. Ahaziah worshipped the god Baal just like his parents, that's all he knew, that's how he was raised, so how could he change his ways if that is all that he knew?

We will move forward in the story so that we can see the Word that God gave Prophet Elijah for Ahab come to pass. Remember God said, 'He would kill the family line when his son becomes king.' That time is now!

King Ahaziah was in the upstairs portion of the palace and was chillin' out and oh boy went to get up and must have lost his balance or was tipsey from drinking too much Royal Red wine. Red wine goes to your head quicker than the white wine, but anyways oh boy went to get up and fell down hard, so hard that he fell straight through the wooden bars that had been placed there to prevent him from falling. Who in the world does something like that? How does that happen?

Once he fell he screamed and hollered like a baby saying, "Help me, somebody come and help me."

One of the servants ran into the area and it was all that he could do to keep from laughing. Remember King Ahaziah was like his mother Evil Queen Boss Jezebel and she thought that everyone was beneath her, so when the servant saw King Ahaziah on the floor hurt and looked around to see broken wood on the floor, believe me it was all that he could do not to laugh out loud! The servant said clearing his throat and holding back laughter, "My King, my King! Are you all right?"

Ahaziah said, "Does it look like I am all right? Help me to my bed and you go and get the doctor for me. Man this is painful! Look at my bone, it looks twisted and it has broken through the skin."

The servant said, "That does look nasty! Okay. Let me help you up and then I will go get the doctor for you."

As soon as the servant left and the door was closed you could hear him running down the hallway screaming in laughter and tears running down his eyes from laughing so hard. One of the other servants said, "Dude what IZ so funny? Why you laughing so hard and crying?"

He said, "Man, I heard King A hollering for help. So I ran in and it was the prettiest sight known to man! He was on the floor and had broken through the wooden rail that was there to keep him from falling. It was all I could do not to laugh in his face."

The other servant said, "Serves his young privileged behind right. Maybe now that he has hurt himself he will think about how he treats us and others. I wish I could have seen it. Run on and get the doctor, I will be sure to spread the word of joy about King A's fall!"

The doctor finally came in to see the King and after a full examination and treating the injured areas he said, "There isn't much more that I can do for you. You really did it this time. I warned you about all of that drinking the last time that I was here and you hurt yourself. Now look at you! All broken up with wood pieces in your open wounds. You have really outdone yourself this time. I would be surprised if you ever get out of that bed again."

Ahaziah said, "DOC! Get out!! What good are you if you can't help your King? You are a doctor and you can't help me of all people. I could see if I were some low peasant out there in the kingdom, but I am your King!!"

Then he turned and told the servant, "Now, I need you to go over to the chapel and ask my god, Baal-Zebub, the god of Ekron, if he knows whether I will get better or not?"

Now the servant was upset and certainly stopped all of that laughing, because he was not a Baal worshipper and didn't want to go in there and ask Baal anything. Just in that moment God heard the commotion and spoke to Prophet Elijah and said, "There is trouble in the palace again. This time it's the son of Ahab and Jezebel. It is time to carry out my word that I gave to Ahab when he tried to take Naboth's vineyard."

Elijah said, "Right, right. I do understand."

God said, "I need you to go to Samaria where King Ahaziah is. He has sent a servant to ask Baal-Zebub a question about his health. I want you to say why are you going to ask Baal-Zebub god of Ekron a question? Why are you not asking the God of Israel? Is it because you don't believe that the God of Israel has the answer or because you can't see a statute of the God of Israel you think that he does not exist? Because you think this, this is what the Lord God of Israel says, 'You will die in that very bed that you are laying in now. You will not get up again!!'

So Elijah went to Samaria and met the servant before he reached the chapel to ask the god of Ekron, Baal-Zebub the question. He told the servant exactly what the Lord said. The servant went back to Ahaziah and Ahaziah said, "You came back too soon. There is no way in this short period of time that you made it to the chapel, asked Baal and made it back here to me! What is the problem?"

The servant said, "Well what had happened was, you see I was on my way and there was a man that met us. It was as if he knew exactly where we were going and why, and I say that because he told us to come back here to you and ask you why are you asking Baal-Zebub a question and not the God of Israel? Don't you think that the God of Israel exists? Just because you think that the God of Israel does not exist because there is no statute of Him, you will not get out of the bed that you are laying in, you will die in that very bed."

Ahaziah said, "Don't even start! What did this man look like? And, why did you take his word and comeback to me without going to see Baal?"

The servant said, "Well, he had on a big thick fur coat with a black leather belt around the waist of the coat. And we came back before asking Baal, because he was so convincing and as we said he knew where we were going and who we were going to see."

Ahaziah said, "Say no more. I know who that man is! It's that Prophet named Elijah. I heard my father talk about him. He is a Tishbite."

Ahaziah continued, "Go tell the Captain of the Royal Army that I need him to go and get Elijah and bring him to me."

The captain gathered 50 of his best men and went to find Elijah. When they found Elijah he was chillin' on the top of a hill. Elijah was enjoying the sky and the serenity. He was enjoying conversation with the Lord.

The captain approached the hill and said to Elijah, "Yo! Yo Elijah! Get down here at once! The king wants to see you and we are not leaving without you. Now we can do this the easy way or the hard way, it's up to you. We don't mind coming up there, beating you within an inch of your life and taking you to the king."

Elijah said, "You are interrupting prime conversation between me and God! I really don't know who you think that you are talking to. You are not the boss of me and I will not do what you say and come down. I have the power of God, because I am God's man, so I say to you that the fire of God will come down from heaven and cremate you and your 50 men. That's right! You thought that you came to bring the heat and smoke to me, well I am bringing the fire of God to you and your 50 measly men. You will burn this day right in front of this hill!"

The captain and his men started to laugh, but with the first giggle, the fire came down and burnt them crispier than a 51 piece family reunion sized chicken bucket!!

After the captain and his 50 men did not come back, Ahaziah sent a second captain and another 50 men and guess what, Elijah lit them up with fire as well. Fried crisp!

Ahaziah just didn't get the message to leave Elijah alone because he sent a 3rd captain with another 50 soldiers. This time when the captain came he saw the burn marks around the base of the hill where the other 102 men had stood. So this captain got smart and spoke to Elijah in a very respectful manner and he even fell on his knees to talk to him. The 3rd captain spoke in almost a Baptist hooping prayer sermon style, "Dear Elijah, man of God, PUH-LEEZE let me and my men live. PUH-LEEZE don't burn us up! PUH-LEEZE!"

You could almost hear the organ backing him up and a few tambourines shaking.

After the captain spoke, or should I say after he prayer preached, the Lord spoke to Elijah and said, "This captain gets it. He understands who you are, who I am and the power that I have given you. Don't burn them up and do not be afraid to go with them. I need you to go see King Ahaziah and personally deliver My word to him yourself."

Prophet Elijah came down off that hill and immediately the 51 men jumped back in fear. They did not know what to expect. Prophet Elijah said to the 3rd captain and his men, "Chill out. If I were going to burn you I didn't have to come down off the hill to do it. Man, you do know that it's a good thing that you came correct, cause had you not come to me with respect you would have been a dark spot in this grass just like these other dark spots! I have plenty of fire to go around for everyone!"

The 3rd captain said, "Oh yes, I wasn't comin' up here talkin' like I don't know who you are. Not me! I KNOW the living God and the power that He has given you. I know who you are and who you represent!"

When Elijah was face to face with Ahaziah he said, "Dude, why did you send your servant to ask Baal-Zebub if you will get better? You did this because you think that the God of Israel is not real. Just ask your 102 men that I fried like a family reunion sized crispy chicken bucket. The God of Israel wants you to know that since you did not come to Him and do not believe in Him you will die right where you are! And that time is NOW!"

The whole time Elijah was speaking Ahaziah was thinking of things that he was going to say like, "Who do you think you are telling my servant to come back here and tell me that I am going to die and where are my 102 men that I sent to get you? You can't tell me what is going to happen to me, only Baal-Zebub will tell me my fate. You are not that man! I will have your head!"

Chile, when I tell you that the word of God happened and it happened with a quickness, it did. Ahaziah didn't get to say a word of what he had been thinking, because as soon as Elijah finished speaking and saying, 'Now!' Ahaziah up and DIED! Gurl, HE DIED right there on his sick bed, just as God spoke through Prophet Elijah!

The servants, the 3rd captain and his 50 men all gasped for air as they saw King Ahaziah die right in front of their eyes at the word of Elijah. They fell all over the floor in fear and started trembling and crying. A few of the soldiers urinated on themselves. I might have done that too after witnessing the Word come to life like that!

Elijah had to tell them, "Y'all can get up. God did not send me here to kill you too, just to deliver a Word of death to Ahaziah. Now get up and take me back to my hill."

Since Ahaziah did not have any sons to take his throne Ahaziah's brother, Joram became King.

I know that you are probably wondering what in the world happened to Queen Jezebel? Well in 2 Kings Chapter 9, Evil Boss Queen Jezebel finally meets her maker.

Jezebel taunted Prophet Elijah and had him so scared that he hid himself away. Why did Elijah hide? He had the power of God to fry people and he delivered God's powerful word to whomever God

said. But he was now sceered of Evil Boss Queen
Jezebel. She was something else.

In 1 Kings 19, that Evil Boss Queen had all
the prophets killed and after doing that she had the
nerve to send a message to Prophet Elijah saying,
"Now you know that I have had all of the God's
prophets killed. I had their heads and by this time
tomorrow I am going to do the same to you. Yes,
PROPHET, I am prophesying your death just like
you did to my son!"

Now I am not sure why Prophet Elijah, the
man that had brought a word of death to King
Ahaziah and who had performed miracles and burnt
men alive was so scared. He had the power of God
on his side, but that didn't seem to cross his mind
because Elijah got so scared that he ran into woods

and hid himself under a tree. Yes, under a tree!! He not only hid under the tree but he asked God to allow him to die right there! I guess the Lord felt sorry for him, because while Elijah was out there hiding under the Broom tree the Lord sent an angel to feed him for forty days and forty nights. Hmmm… forty days and forty nights sounds so familiar, if not check out Luke 4:2 when the devil tempted Jesus for forty days and forty nights!!

When Elijah left the tree he found a cave to hide in and while he was there the Lord had a lengthy conversation with him and told him, "Dude, what are you doing hiding out in a cave? The tree was bad enough, but now you are in a damp cave with bats."

Elijah said, "Lord I am sceered! I know that you know what has happened to all of the other prophets. That demon Evil Boss Queen Jezebel has killed and beheaded them all! The people have torn down Your altars, destroyed Your places of worship so I had to run and hide in order to save my life!"

God replied, "Man go outside! Stand out there and watch as I pass by."

This scenario of the Lord passing by will happen again in Exodus 34:6 when Moses asked the Lord to show him His glory. I will cover that in a future book to come.

As the Lord passed by there was a powerful wind that came and caused the mountains to shake and break. Elijah thought that the powerful wind was the Lord passing by, but it was not. Then a strong earthquake came, fire and a small whisper was heard. Elijah thought to himself, "If the Lord was not in the wind, the earthquake or fire, this small voice must be Him!"

So when Elijah heard this small voice, speaking so calmly and peacefully he knew it was God and he put his hoody up on his head and around his face, went outside and heard the Lord say again, "Elijah! Dude what are you doing here?"

Elijah repeated the same thing that he said earlier, "Lord I am sceered! I know that you know what has happened to all of the other prophets. That demon Boss Queen Jezebel has killed and beheaded them all! The people have torn down Your altars, destroyed Your places of worship so I had to run and hide in order to save my life!"

God said to Elijah, "Get out of this cave and go to Damascus and anoint Hazael as king over Syria, then anoint Jehu as king over Israel and then anoint Elisha as prophet in your place. These kings will straighten out the current sit-chu-mation with Evil Boss Queen Jezebel. If any of those Baal worshippers escape from Evil Boss Queen Jezebel's area then King Hazael and his men will get them, and if any escape King Hazael then King Jehu and his men shall kill them and if any of them escape King Hazael and King Jehu, then Prophet Elisha will catch them on the tail end and kill them. After all of this, there will only be seven thousand left in Israel that have not bowed their knees to Baal and that have not kissed Baal. I am only leaving seven thousand alive to worship me. Seven is My number for completion, so these seven thousand will mark the end of the reign of Baal Worship!"

So Prophet Elijah left the cave and found Elisha out in a field working like a slave. He had twelve ox and was plowing a field. When Prophet Elijah passed by Elisha he simply flung his fur coat around where Elisha was working. Immediately the power of God hit Elisha and he dropped that plow and ran to Elijah. In that moment Elisha knew that he had to leave his parent's home and follow Elijah. Elisha asked. "Please let me go and tell my mom and dad goodbye. I just want to let them know what has happened and that I must follow the call of God on my life."

Elijah said, "If after what I have done to you and for you, you want to go to speak to your mom and dad, then go on back and do what ya gotta do. I am going to keep it movin' because I have other things to do."

Elisha went back and took the 12 oxen that he was plowing with and turned them into some oxtail soup and gave it to everyone that was in his little town. That was something to see and I bet it was some good oxtail soup. After the party was over and he talked with his parents Elisha took off to find where Elijah went.

After the war broke out between King Hazael, King Jehu and Syria, Jehu had a specific assignment from God and that was to kill the royal family. It was Jehu that shot the arrow that killed

King Ahab when he was in battle and as he did the Lord showed Jehu the blood of Neboth.

Jehu went to Jezreel and when the Evil Boss Queen Jezebel heard about him pullin' up she thought that she would make herself pretty and look out of a window. I know that she didn't think she could seduce King Jehu and I just know that she really couldn't have thought that make-up and lip stick would help that face! She had nothing to entice him with because he was all about his assignment, which meant she was about to die.

Evil Boss Queen Jezebel looked down and said to King Jehu, "Hey there? Is your name peace, Zimri, the one who murdered King Ahab, my man!?"

Jehu said to himself, "Man, I don't have time for this witch and all of the ra-ra nonsense that she is speaking!"

Then he shouted out, "Who is ridin' with me?"

Two men that were in the palace with Jezebel heard Jehu and looked out the window. These two men had been castrated, against their will, to serve the Evil Boss Queen and the spineless wussy king who was killed in battle by Jehu's arrow. These two men decided that they would have Jehu's back. When Jehu saw them he said, "If you ridin' with me, then throw that Evil Queen Boss witch out of the window."

The two men were more than happy to do so. They thought to themselves, "This Evil Boss Queen witch took my manhood and made me serve her and the others against my will. She had me around all of those pretty ladies and I didn't even have anything to offer them and still do not! It's time for that evil demonic Boss Queen to have a meeting with the concrete."

They ran over to Jezebel and she said, "Wait, wait. What are you doing? Put me down, put me down!"

The two men said, "We are not only going to put you down, we are going to throw you down, so that you can be on time for your meeting with the concrete. You treated us like dirt, so it is time for you to go and become like dirt. Ashes to ashes and dirt to dirt! "

So they tossed her old wicked, wrinkled up behind out of the window. When she hit the ground her blood and brains splattered all over the palace wall and the horses that were passing by ran right over her like she was road kill. And yes, the dogs showed up and licked her blood and the birds ate her flesh just as God said it would happen.

Jehu acted as if nothing significant happened because he went into a nearby restaurant and sat down and had a meal and something to drink. He and his men were having a meal of celebration. The two men that threw her out of the window came down and joined in on the celebration.

After Jehu ate and drank he told his men, "Ok now you can go out there and get that witch up off the ground and bury her somewhere, she is a king's daughter so I will show at least one ounce of respect."

The men went outside but the only thing that they could find was her skull, feet and the palms of her hands. They ran back into the restaurant to tell King Jehu what had happened and he said, "Well that's the Word of God being fulfilled. The Lord spoke through Prophet Elijah to King Ahab that the dogs would eat her to the point of nothing being left. Now no one can say 'Here lies Evil Queen Boss Jezebel."

WOW! What a befitting ending for the Evil Queen Boss Jezebel!

Point (s) to Ponder: Why did Ahab let Jezebel act on his behalf? He knew that she was going to do something evil and manipulative to get him the vineyard? Why was Naboth so quick to accept the invitation to lead out the day of fasting rather than ask the Lord if he should accept? Do you think that Ahaziah could have changed his ways from how his parents Ahab and Jezebel raised him? Best question of this story is why was Prophet Elijah so scared of Jezebel when he had the power to literally burn men up on sight?

Take Away: We have just witnessed two incidents of men not asking the Lord what should they do and the end results of them not asking was death, do you think that this applies to us? Should we always ask the Lord what to do? Does this apply to us even though we are now living in modern times?

Prayer: Father we thank You today that You have guidance and wisdom waiting for us, all that we have to do is ask You.

www.ingramcontent.com/pod-product-compliance
Lightning Source LLC
Chambersburg PA
CBHW070458050426
42449CB00012B/3034